A JOURNEY ACROSS ICELAND

The Ministry of
Rev. Jon Sveinsson S.J.

by Rev. Jon Sveinsson, S.J.

Edited by John C. Wilhelmsson

A Journey Across Iceland

Modern English Edition

Copyright © 2014

by John C. Wilhelmsson

ISBN: 0988656396
ISBN-13: 978-0988656390

Chaos To Order Publishing

San Jose, CA

www.c2op.com

CONTENTS

EDITOR'S PREFACE

I have sought for a literary, rather than a literal, translation while attempting to preserve the flow of the original narrative. Many chapter breaks have been added in order to give the reader a chance to reflect upon the rich writing and pure descriptions of Iceland. Old English words like "cope" (a religious vestment) have been updated to "cloak." Yet at the same time I have made no effort to update Icelandic names or place names. My hope is that the modern reader can understand and enjoy the text while still having the feeling that they are being taken to another place and time.

When Jon Sveinsson wrote this travelogue in 1894 there is no way he could have known of the great fame he would one day acquire as a writer. In fact, it was not until some twenty years later that his classic children's book "Lost in the Arctic" (which in reality should be called "Lost in the Fjord") was first published.

What followed was one of the most improbable and wonderful writing careers one could imagine. Book after book was published and the fame of "Nonni" (Jon Sveinsson's boyhood Icelandic nickname) spread so far and wide that his books were eventually translated into some 40 languages.

This current work, however, is less about "Nonni" and more about the Reverend Jon Sveinsson S. J. A priest of the Society of Jesus who had a long and fruitful ministry worthy of note long before his fame as an author. Like many of his Jesuit brothers,

Reverend Jon Sveinsson was an educator as well as a priest. And indeed this current work shows him as both in all his glory.

The premise of the story is simple: Jon Sveinsson is the only Jesuit priest ever born in Iceland. He left his homeland as a boy, with his beloved brother Armann (or "Manni"), to follow their mutual call to become Jesuit missionaries. Although Manni has since passed on during his studies, Nonni is now the Reverend Jon Sveinsson S. J.

The boys had wished to become missionaries, like St. Francis Xavier, yet Jon Sveinsson has spent most of his time since joining the Jesuits as either a student, and now an instructor, in academia. Still longing to fulfill his dream to become a missionary he has volunteered to travel to Iceland in order to care for the souls of his fellow countrymen. And now, after some amount of time, that call is about to be received.

So here, entirely from the "Public Domain," Chaos To Order Publishing is proud to present "A Journey Across Iceland." Truly a work that the public should have access to for it is both a fine story in itself, and a must read for all those who have enjoyed the "Nonni" books and now wish to know their author better as a person. However, one can never really know an Icelander until one knows their land and culture. And the descriptions of them found here are, in my opinion, some of the finest ever put to page.

John C. Wilhelmsson

COPENHAGEN

CHAPTER ONE

THE CALL RECIEVED

In June, 1894, the welcome news reached me at the College of Ordrupshoj, near Copenhagen Denmark, that Bishop d 'Euch had decided to send me, during my summer vacation, to the Faroe Islands and to Iceland, in order to carry the consolations of our holy religion to the few Catholics who live there. He selected me because I am the only native priest of that country and had always desired to be a missionary among my own people.

I was first to go to Reykjavik to look after some property belonging to the Catholic Mission, and then to cross the country on horseback from the southwest to the north that I might visit, at Ofjord, the only Catholic family living at present in Iceland. The steamer "Thyra" was to take me back to Copenhagen about the beginning of September.

A pupil of our college at Ordrupshoj, anxious to travel during his vacation, asked leave of his parents in order to accompany me. This was the more readily granted, as the boy deserved an unusual reward for having so diligently applied himself to his studies during the whole year that he carried off the first prize of his class on Commencement day.

On the sixth of July, 1894, at 9 O'clock in the morning we boarded the ship "Botnia" of the Asiatic Company. It was to be her maiden trip to Iceland. The first class passengers numbered fifty-three and proved a quaint agglomeration, as there were representatives from America, England, Germany, France, Denmark, Russia, Iceland and the Faroes. From morning to night we could hear five or six different languages spoken, and sometimes a mixture of them all. We soon made one another's acquaintance and from the first we formed one big family, whose union and cordiality increased daily.

The first time we assembled in the dining hall, Frederick, my young companion, and I found ourselves opposite a lady of imposing demeanor. Beside her sat a boy of about nine years, who looked very intelligent. My neighbor, who knew them, informed me that they were the wife and son of the Governor of Iceland. They were returning to their home after a short stay in Copenhagen. Frederick was only twelve years old and he and Magnus, for thus the little Icelander was called, soon became playmates and vowed each other everlasting friendship. The mother of this charming boy showed herself very amiable to us. She insisted on my speaking Icelandic with her for practice. For I was rather rusty in expressing myself in my mother tongue.

On the third day we arrived at Edinburgh, our first resting place. As the steamer was to remain twenty-four hours in the port, Fredrick and I started without delay for the residence of our fellow Jesuits at Lauriston Street, where the Rector, a brother of Admiral Whyte, received us with touching kindness and urged us to spend the night. The following morning he accompanied us to town to buy the necessary provisions for our journey across an almost deserted country. A large box was soon filled with a quantity of canned food, including everything necessary for our sustenance during the time we would have to spend in Iceland far from any dwelling.

The voyage from Edinburgh to the Faroe Isles was most agreeable. Towards evening we reached Thorshavn, the capital and seat of Government of the Faroe Isles, a city void of all interest for a traveler. It had a special interest for me, however, as at Hvidenaes, about an hour's walk from Thorshavn, dwelt the only Catholic of the Islands—a matron about eighty-seven years old. I was to pay her a visit and hurry back before the steamer would continue her route, which would be during the night.

The "Botnia" had cast anchor at some distance, but was surrounded by a number of small boats immediately. I asked the strongest of the boatmen who had come on deck, whether one of them would now row me to Hvidenaes. They answered to a man, that it was impossible, as the currents along this coast were treacherous and the waves beat the shore with great fury. In fact from the steamer we could perceive all along the coast the white breakers. I had, therefore, no other choice than to land at Thorshavn, and there procure a guide to accompany me across the mountain to the house of the poor old lady who desired to see me.

I engaged the first boat near the steamer, and on landing at Thorshavn, I met a little boy from Hvidenaes who offered himself as a guide, so without delay I started on my journey. It is impossible to give an idea of the joy this visit caused the good lady for she had been longing to see a priest. Her copious tears proved a thousand times more eloquent than any words she might have uttered. I was deeply moved at the sight, and I much regretted not to be able to stay with her more than an hour but promised her a longer visit, in two months, on my return from Iceland. It was past midnight when we started our journey to meet the steamer at Thorshavn. The solitary walk, in the half daylight of a boreal night, is one which I shall never forget.

FAROE STAMP OF THYRA STEAMER

CHAPTER TWO

MAKING FOR ICELAND

Early in the morning we steamed off for Iceland and soon began to realize that the inhabited portion of the globe was receding. No ships are seen in these parts—as far as the eye can reach nothing but endless solitude. However, all signs of life did not disappear. Immense whales began to show themselves on the surface of the blue waters and increased in numbers the nearer we approached the North Pole. Now one alone would emerge from the deep, and swimming beside the steamer, would regard with astonishment the monstrous structure, and diving back vanish beneath the water. Then shoals of them would leisurely go through the same routine, much to the astonishment of the passengers, who never grew wary of gazing at so novel a spectacle.

After a sail of two days the rugged and irregular coast of Iceland was clearly perceived, and, as from the waves, arose from our eyes the gigantic snow-capped Oraefa Jökull. This is the loftiest volcano of Iceland; owning to our course we had no opportunity to examine it closely. The steamer passed beyond it, continuing its westerly route. Again land was lost sight of, to reappear soon under quite a different aspect; for now enormous, bare and rugged groups of rocks emerged from the water's surface, and in the background were seen numerous volcanoes side-by-side—known as the Myrdale Jökull, Botn Jökull, the Gotalands Jökull, the Tarfa Jökull, and many others. It was a striking spectacle, although bleak and dreary. We hurriedly passed before the Hjörleifshöfde, a huge pile of solitary rocks along the dreary coast; on each side of this colossus extends a barren desert, the Myrdalsander, bounded on the right by the swift current of the Kutafijöt. From its bank stretched a great meadow with a dark spot in the middle; it is the Thikkvaboers Kloster, formerly a Catholic monastery, now an isolated farm in the midst of this desert.

Behind the rocks extends a road which it is dangerous to enter on account of the numerous quagmires. It is said that some travelers, in spite of warnings, once ventured to ride alone along this road, but neither they nor their ponies were ever heard of afterward.

We have already left in our rear the Hjörleipshöfde. The change of the scenery is striking. We are at Portland, its real name being Dyrh61acy. It is a long projecting cape, in front of which, at a short distance from the shore, rises a lofty and steep rock, shaped so as to make a natural gateway, whence its name of Portland. Our steamer might have easily passed under the arches of this natural vault. A shoal of whales made their appearance on our left. They no longer excited the admiration of the passengers, so absorbed were we in contemplating the marvelous spectacle on the side of the land. It was a sight altogether new for most of us, and beside these gigantic mountains what a small and insignificant thing the largest whale appeared! It was already eight O'clock in the evening and the sun still shone in all its brilliancy. In this latitude it sets but for a short time behind the dazzling glaciers which spread out on our right.

We steered again towards the high sea, and were greeted by an unexpected sight. Straight ahead of us, at a distance of fifty miles, we beheld a group of isles of blackish rock formation, they are the Westman Isles; which, in 1627, met such a sad fate. They were attacked by Algerian pirates; the church and all the principal buildings were burned to the ground; 250 islanders were carried off into slavery; all the rest were wantonly put to the sword.

This was to be our first stop in Iceland, and we expected to reach port about 1 O'clock A. M. It was a sail of five hours and the passengers were willing to spend this time on deck, but the sudden rising of a thick fog threw a veil over the scenery.

They retired reluctantly therefore to their berths. Frederick followed the crowd; as for myself I could not make up my mind to leave the deck, but kept pacing up and down, revolving in my mind the superb sights of which nature has been so lavish in this part of the globe. I was amply rewarded for my watching; after two hours a light wind sprang up, which, in a few moments, chased the dense mist away. A magnificent spectacle suddenly appeared before me, which greatly surpassed all I had seen till now. Straight ahead of us, at a mile's distance, lie the Westmann Isles; on the right, shone the glittering splendor of a group of glaciers, illumined by the evening sun. The nearest is the formidable EyjafjallaJökull; in the background at a greater distance towers mount Hekla, the best known volcano of Iceland. As far as the eye can reach huge drifts of snow and mountains of ice appear enveloped in a sheet of living flame, while the whole northwest horizon resembles a vast ocean of fire in which are seen the richest tints of gold and purple. Thus flooded with light, these glacial solitudes looked cheering enough; this dreary and death-like clime, which in truth is often so sad to behold, presented a most brilliant aspect. The sight was too grand not to be enjoyed by all. The passengers were therefore called from dreamland, so that on our arrival at the Westmann Isles, all were on deck; it was 1 O'clock A.M. The houses, which we readily perceived, were clustered together at the foot of Mount Eyjafjalla. You imagine they are going to be crushed by the enormous mass that hangs over them. This superb spectacle produced a vivid impression on all present. Two Germans especially vented their enthusiasm, exclaiming, "We have crossed Switzerland in every direction; we have visited the fiords of Norway, but nowhere have we met with a sight like this."

Each one retired to his berth to enjoy a good sleep after the many impressions of this memorable day. The next day we arose just as the steamer entered the bay of

Faxafiord, which has a width of fifty miles
from cape to cape. At its extreme end lies
Reykjavik. The weather was superb. At
some distance we could distinctly see the
Snefell covered with snow and ice; this
volcano, well-known in the history of
Iceland, is at present extinct. On a line with
the city runs the majestic range of the Esja
Mountains dazzling the beholder with their
whiteness. As we steamed up the bay we
passed along a number of inhabited islands
covered with verdure, and surrounded by a
channel so deep that the largest ship can
pass between them and the coast. There
were many steamers lying in the harbor, the
most conspicuous of which was the French
man-of-war "Nielly,"—which still bore
marks of the balls it received during the
Tonkin war, and further up, the Danish
frigate "Diana." The numerous merchant
ships did not attract our attention.

The French man-of-war is stationed here
to watch over and protect a flotilla of fishing
boats, which leave the ports of France every

year for Iceland to fish for the cod. About 5000 Frenchmen live thus in Iceland during the summer months, supporting themselves from the natural resources of the island. Besides there is a numerous Norwegian, English, American, and cosmopolitan contingent. This lucrative fishing brings a large sum to the pockets of these strangers. The poor Icelander has, up to the present, been wanting in means to draw profit on any great scale from these treasures which surround him.

REYKJAVIK

CHAPTER THREE

AT REYKJAVIK

Reykjavik resembles a small Norwegian city; it numbers about 4000 inhabitants. As soon as we were anchored, a swarm of row boats surrounded the steamer. Frederick and I hurried to engage one; the owner, a young man, treated us with the utmost politeness; he himself lowered our baggage into the boat. As we glided along, he plied me with a number of questions, which anywhere else would be considered impertinent, but it seems to be here the custom of the country, and everyone is oblige to undergo this strange examination.

I had to tell him my name and that of Frederick, what we were, where we came from, where we were going, for what purpose, and so forth. When he learned that I was a Catholic priest on my way to Ofjord he exclaimed, "0 indeed, you are going to pay a visit to Gunnar Einarsson; he is Catholic, his son is at college here in Reykjavik;" our arrival at the wharf brought the conversation to an end. On landing I wished to pay the young man, but he steadily refused any remuneration for such a slight service. He procured us a porter to carry our baggage and showed us the way to the hotel Reykjavik where we intended to stop.

The hotel is a large framed building situated in the principle street in the city. The owner, Mrs. Zaega, is a native of Iceland; she spent several years in England to learn English and cooking, and profited very much by her residence in that country, especially with regard to the former accomplishment. All the comforts enjoyed in a similar establishment can be had here and everything is arranged as in Europe. This is true of all the houses of well-to-do people; so that the city presented nothing which deserves special mention.

Two items may prove of interest to my readers. The first is my visit to the French man-of-war "Nielly." The day after my arrival I hired a boat to take me to the "Nielly," hoping to find a chaplain on board, but I was disappointed. I found, however, 300 men, most of them Catholics. At a second visit, I was able to see the captain of the ship and obtain from him—an unusual thing—permission for his men to visit me on shore, and to attend to their religious duties. During ten days I received daily visits from the cadets and officers, many of whom received Holy Communion. On the eve of the departure of the man-of-war the captain came himself to thank me for the services I had rendered to his men. He assured me that he valued them most highly.

The second item worthy of notice was my visit to the cathedral, now in the hands of Lutherans. The sacristan, after having shown me through the edifice, led me to a small room near the entrance. There he opened an old wardrobe and drew from it a very rich and beautiful cloak, but so old that the parts hardly hung together. I carefully examined the venerable relic. Was I mistaken? I saw figures of saints delicately embroidered in gold on a field of red silk, all of exquisite taste. It was indeed a relic of Old Catholic times. The sacristan informed me that this cloak had been sent by the Pope about 1550 to Jon Arason, the last martyred bishop of Iceland. "But what use do you now make of it?" I asked. He replied, "Once a year our bishop wears it, when he ordains new ministers. This custom dates from time immemorial." This fact is true. Pope Paul III sent this present to Jon Arason as a token of esteem for the zeal he had displayed in the cause of religion. Two years later, in 1552, the bishop was captured and beheaded by the Danish reformers. It is interesting to notice with what veneration the Protestants of this far-off island have preserved this precious souvenir of a Pope!

I must not forget to mention here that during our whole stay at Reykjavik, the

Governor and his lady showed us the greatest kindness. They often let us use their best ponies to go on excursions in the neighborhood. Young Magnus acted as our guide and one of their servants on horseback followed at a short distance, to render us any service we might need. In this manner we visited many very interesting spots, among others the spring of boiling water, where the soiled linen of Reykjavik are washed. We forded several rivers, and learned to strike out in different paths, for there are no roads in Iceland. This proved a good preparation for our excursion across the country.

All strangers, who in one way or another become acquainted with the Governor, cannot help praising his courtesy and noble manners. Moreover, wherever we went, people always showed us great kindness, and were ever happy to give us the information we asked for. Thus I learned many useful things about managing our horses, about the clothing and provisions we required, the different routes we were to take, the farms we were to stop at in preference to others, and so forth. The route of our trip was so fully traced out that we could undertake it without the least fear, and we needed no guide except for some dangerous passes. Nowhere was payment for services asked. One day I had a small toy repaired by a goldsmith; when I wished to pay him he said he could not accept anything for such a trifle. Two lads, who rowed us to the "Nielly," likewise refused the money I offered them. These good people would believe themselves degraded if they accepted the least remuneration for the little services they render with such good will.

At last the time came for us to start on our trip; the last preparations for the journey had to be made. It was like crossing a great desert, for we had not only to consider the immense distance to be covered—Iceland is much larger than Ireland—but also the primitive way of making this long journey. Railways and carriage roads are altogether unknown here. Travelling is done, as in the days of Arild, on the back of Icelandic ponies. Moreover, once out of the capital, you find yourself immediately out of civilization—no hotels, no mile-post, no roads, sometimes not even the least sign of a path, and no bridges to cross the rivers except in one or two places.

Before undertaking a journey through such a country, it is easily understood how necessary it was to make careful preparations. Our first concern was to purchase horses, as it is preferable to buy them, and dispose of them after the expedition. Accordingly, I begged a merchant, whom I knew, to purchase for us three strong and gentle ponies. He promised to do his best to please us, and he kept his word. Our little ponies were charming in every respect; and the further we advanced the more attached we became to them, as they rendered us such good service. I had them shod anew, and I procured some horseshoes and nails, in case of accident. I bought two saddles, a pack saddle, three horse bits, two whips, and two solid boxes for our provisions and other objects we had to take along. The price of all amounted to seventeen crowns. Our trunks were sent by steamer from Reykjavik to Akureyri. We were likewise obliged to procure oilcloth suits, waterproof hats, overcoats, and boots; we added to the provisions we bought at Edinburgh some canned meats, preserves, cakes, biscuits and cocoa, which proved of great service. All these articles cost no more than in England.

To pack the boxes is an art which can only be acquired by practice. They have to be arranged in such a way that the weight is the same on each side of the saddle; every article must be tightly packed so that nothing can move when they are shaken by the lively trot of the pony. An Englishman told me that, from neglect of this, the very first day his cakes and biscuits were reduced to crumbs. Our itinerary was traced beforehand as exactly as possible. My

pocketbook was full of notes and marks of
the paths, the rivers, the bogs, the
quagmires, the mountains, the lakes, the
swamps, and the farmhouses.

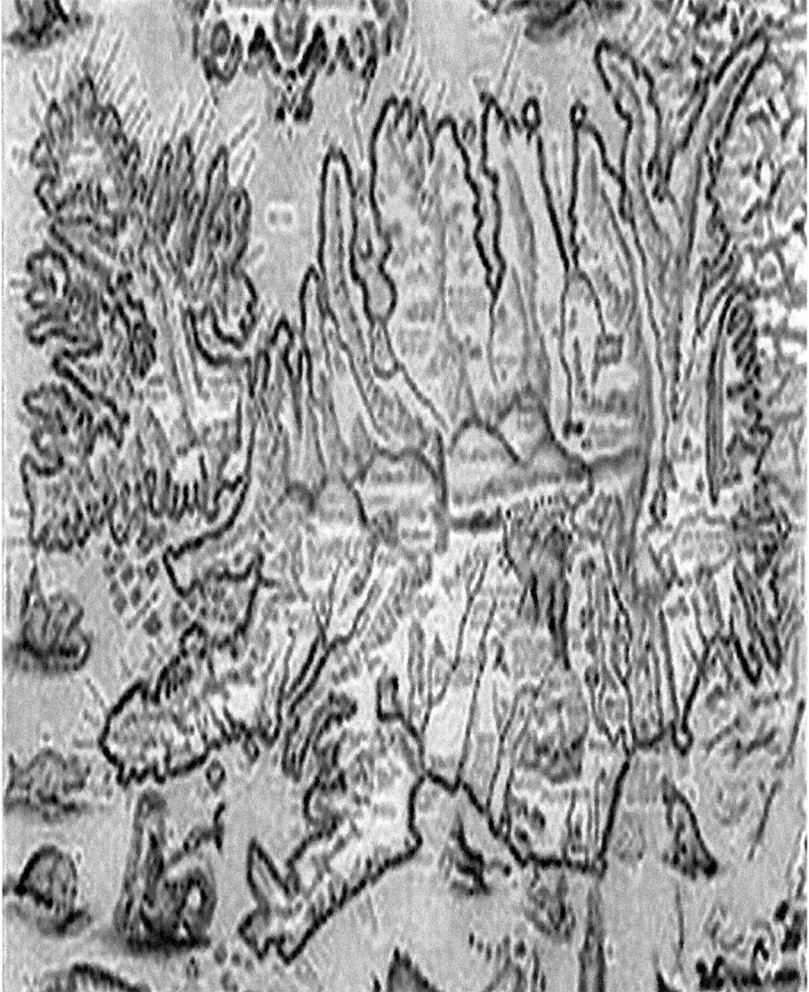

CHAPTER FOUR

THE JOURNEY ACROSS BEGINS

We started from Reykjavik on July 29 at 1 O'clock P.M. after having bid farewell to our many friends. A servant of the hotel accompanied us to the outskirts of the city and then we were left to ourselves and our good angels. We have now bid good bye, for some time, to the civilized world, to all modern civilization with its comforts and discomforts; here we are alone with God's free and pure nature. Henceforth we are to mingle with people whose tongue, manners, customs and dwellings are such as they were 1000 years ago. The people of Iceland may very correctly be styled an anachronism in the nineteenth century they live and speak as they did in the remotest times. The only thing modern in their dwellings is the room or parlor for strangers which is a part of every farmhouse nowadays; but for this improvement we would have had to carry a tent and hammocks, as many English tourists do; but this requires another pack horse. We proceeded at a lively pace, and after a ride of two hours we lost sight of the sea. Our course lay now to the interior of the country which we were to cross from south to north. At a distance ahead of us, and lost in the clouds, rose chains of black mountains; many days were required to reach them, and when there we were to be in complete wilderness. This thought produced a strange feeling of loneliness. The temperature was very mild, the sky pure and cloudless, it was a beautiful summer day. "This is what I call travelling," exclaimed my little companion, "it is so different from being locked up in narrow compartments of the railway cars. What a fresh and delicious climate!" We went on as quickly as possible although we could not count on covering a great distance that day, as we left Reykjavik too late, and we had several unavoidable delays.

Suddenly the horses pricked up their ears; something unusual ahead of us must have attract their attention. In fact, we soon caught sight of a curious caravan—some twenty horses drawn up in one long file, the head of each being tied to the tail of the one immediately before him; a mounted boy in the van led the cavalcade. In the rear a group of peasants, also mounted, followed.

They had been at Reykjavik, and were on their way home. Each horse carried on his back a heavy burden of diverse articles; it reminded me of a primitive freight train. Thus they transport sacks of wheat, farm seeds, boxes of sugar, coffee, tobacco, and so on—even beams, rafters, lumber and other building materials. This caravan proceeded quietly and regularly, although now and then one of the horses becoming unruly, pulled somewhat too roughly the tail of the one before him, and thus caused a temporary confusion. These caravans pick their way in a marvelous manner through the winding paths, and cross with astonishing ease the rivers and torrents; often they have to make over a hundred miles to reach the nearest town. Of course they carry their tents with them on the backs of their horses. In the evening they select a comfortable camping place in some large prairie to spend the night, and the horses are let free to browse.

When we approached the rear of the caravan, the men stopped and saluted us according to the custom of the country: "Saelir veriel per!" namely, "Be ye blessed!" We answered in the same manner. Then came the customary questions which travelling Icelanders exchange when they meet. "What is your name? Your profession? Where do you come from? Where are you going?" and so on. In brief, one has to undergo a regular examination. When mutual curiosity has been satisfied, they separate with a last, "Be ye blessed!" and continue their journey, each one in his own direction.

All at once we heard the sound of hoofs in the rear. We looked back and were astonished to see a little boy on horseback making for us at full speed. When he was near us, he stopped, took off his hat and saluted us, saying, "Be ye blessed!" We answered in the same manner. Then the conversation started, beginning with the usual examination, which is never omitted. In my turn I questioned him: "What is your name?" He replied, "Thorston." How old are you?" "Ten." "Where are you going?"" "Nowhere in particular; I am out for amusement." "Where do you come from?"" "Reykjavik." "Whose pony do you ride?" "My father's." "How far are you going?" "I will accompany you for some time, then I will return home. Give me the bridle of your pack horse, I will lead him for you." I willingly accepted the offer and we rode side by side talking on different subjects. Frederick could already understand Icelandic, and the boy asked him many questions. He wished to know how people travel in Denmark, and was delighted to hear about wagons, big horses, tall trees, and the thousand marvels of our dear

Copenhagen. "Oh how I should like to live in your country, what fun you must have!" exclaimed the little Icelander. We had soon to part. Frederick gave the boy a beautiful picture which seemed to please him exceedingly. He thanked him, after the manner of Icelandic children, by shaking hands. He bade us farewell; we wished him a happy journey and off he went at full gallop in the direction of Reykjavik. You will never meet a foot traveler in the whole of Iceland; everybody knows how to ride on horseback.

As the sun was nearing the mountain crests, we distinguished at a distance the farm of "Middlar," where we expected to spend the night. On the right we saw three large lakes between two chains of mountains. They were many miles distant from one another. On the left were the Esja Mountains, which spread to Reykjavik; along these we were to ride the whole of the following day. It was about 9 O'clock P. M., and the sun shone as at midday. We soon reached the height above the farm, and we beheld at our feet the house surrounded by luxuriant prairies, where, at a short distance, the mowers were still at work. We had to descend the declivity slowly and carefully as it was so steep that we had to lean backwards to avoid falling down headlong. Finally we reached a small paved yard in front of the house; the farmer had noticed our arrival and had come to meet us. We exchanged the usual salutations and I asked him: "May we spend the night with you?" "Certainly" said he, "Please dismount."

CHAPTER FIVE

AT MIDDLAR FARM

He ran to the entrance of the house and cried out, "Helgi!" A young lad immediately appeared, took our horses, and began without delay to remove the saddle. I wished to help him to take down the boxes, but the farmer would not allow it. "Do not worry," said he, "we will take care of your baggage; you must be tired after your journey, please follow me to the house where you will find rest." We went with him through a long and dark corridor, lined on either side with stout joists which kept the mud walls together. They seemed to have been there for centuries.

Soon we turned to the right into another dark passage. Our kind host warned us of some steps which we ascended carefully; then he opened a door and said, "Here is your room!" We entered an apartment in which we found everything tastefully and comfortably arranged. The wainscoting was new; there was a wardrobe and a mahogany bureau, a soft lounge, and in the centre of the room an elegant little round table. At the lower end stood a large bedstead of antique form, and a new harmonium! The walls were decorated with paintings and richly framed pictures.

Our baggage was immediately brought to our room; at the same time the farmer's daughter came to ask us what we desired for supper. I handed her a box of canned meat and told her to put it in boiling water for a quarter of an hour. When this was done we sat down to an excellent meal, our host furnishing us with delicious bread and fresh milk. After supper I went to see how our ponies were doing. I found them on a meadow at a short distance from the house. They were so busily engaged browsing the tender grass that they did not even raise their heads to look at me.

Poor creatures! It is an indispensable condition of their existence to profit, as much as possible, by these few hours of rest; to eat their fill and thus prepare themselves for the fatigues of the next day. Their work is often above their strength and they succumb on the way, as is proved by the numerous skeletons that we afterwards met on our journey. While walking in the prairie, I perceived that whenever the horses changed place they leaped in a rather curious fashion. On examining them I discovered that the farmer had, according to custom, tied their fore-feet together lest they should return to Reykjavik during the night. I greatly desired to procure them a more comfortable rest, but I could not interfere.

I hurried back to the house to enjoy a much needed rest after so fatiguing a day. The good farmer kept us company for a while. He eagerly inquired about the news of the capital and of foreign lands. The Icelanders of today are as desirous of news as were their ancestors in years gone by.

They say that formerly it was no unusual event to see an important and noisy assembly break up at once when they heard that a ship had moored in a neighboring harbor: everyone ran to hear the news. I asked our host where he had bought the elegant harmonium. "I did not buy it," he replied, "my son made it." "But how is it possible?" I said in astonishment. "My son has been at Reykjavik," continued the farmer, "there he studied an instrument in all its details and on his return he spent his leisure hours manufacturing a similar one." Could you ever imagine that a simple peasant lad, living on an isolated farm, would be able to construct a harmonium by no means inferior in art and perfection to those made by well-known manufacturers? We were at our wits' end, when we were further informed that he had moreover learned, without master, to play on his instrument. The following morning he executed, very well indeed, several Danish and Icelandic melodies; and sang with much feeling. It seems that in the interior of the country many farmers are in possession of even larger and better made harmoniums than the one we saw—all the work of their sons! A young man in the North has made a reputation for himself in this kind of workmanship, and he has already made presents of several instruments to the farmers of his neighborhood. We had the pleasure, later on, of seeing one of these harmoniums in the farmhouse at "Modrvollum," at Ofjord. It is so perfect in its every detail that no one could guess where and by whom it was manufactured.

We slept profoundly during the whole night; the beds, the coverlets, everything was so exquisitely neat and comfortable. In the morning our kind hostess brought us, on a tray, hot coffee and rolls. Shortly afterwards we went to see how our ponies had spent the night. We found them still grazing, but with less avidity than in the evening. One of them had broken the rope that bound his feet but even then—through force of habit—he continued as before to advance leaping, although he was no longer fettered. The good hostess prepared a sumptuous breakfast of all the best things she had to offer; it was followed by another cup of coffee. This is indeed the national drink, and the saying is true—"If you wish to know what coffee is, go to Iceland." Coffee is taken at least three time a day, and whenever you stop on a journey, you are invited to partake of a delicious cup of this beverage.

Breakfast over, we prepared, without delay, to resume our journey, for between Middlar and Thingvalla, where we hoped to spend the night, there is not a single habitation, and along the whole road nothing is seen on either side but lofty mountains covered with snow and ice. As a thick fog hung over the meadows, we put on the rubber suits we had provided for such contingencies. On the point of starting, I wished to pay for our board; but our host positively declined to take any remuneration, saying that he never accepted payment for

hospitality tendered to his countrymen. As I
steadily insisted, he accepted a paltry sum.
He accompanied us a certain distance, and
we parted.

THINGVALLA

CHAPTER SIX

BOUND FOR THINGVALLA

For hours the landscape presented a wild aspect, until we reached the "Selja" valley, which was covered with a fresh and vivid green. We forded five or six rivers and torrents. When we reached the foot of the Mossfellshoj we stopped for a short time to rest ourselves and to give our horses a chance to taste the fresh grass, which abounded there. Poor little animals! They needed refreshment, for soon they were to exert all their strength to climb the mountain before us. The ascent is tiresome, and there is not a blade of grass to greet their eyes during a long and wearisome pull. We bathed the backs of our horses before replacing the saddles, and then started. When we reached the top of the mountain we beheld a wild and striking panorama. On the left were the snow-crowned Esja Mountains; on the right immense black mountains of fantastic shapes formed from base to crest of innumerable boulders of lava—relics of the glacial period—broken up and thrown at random in the strangest confusion. Before us stretched the great plateau of the Mossfellshoj, with a path winding through it as far as the eye could reach. This was to be our direction for many a mile.

Some years ago eight persons were travelling here in the midst of winter. They were overtaken in this unlucky spot by a violent snow blizzard, and losing their way all perished. It is since this accident, that the road has been put in its present condition; for now a line of sign posts, ten or twelve feet high, erected along the road, point out its direction. These silent but indispensable guides, look like so many spectres stretching a thin arm over the road in sign of warning. After a ride of two hours, we arrived at the middle of the plateau. There we saw almost bordering the road a strange building which provoked sad reflections.

It is built of thick stone walls with no windows, the only entrance being a wooden door, surmounted by a large wooden cross. Here the travelers take refuge when they cross the mountain in winter and are overtaken by a storm. Naturally enough the thought of the eight victims who perished so miserably, for lack of such a refuge, stole over our minds. We hurried on at a rapid pace, for it was cool on the heights, and we had two more hours to ride before we could begin the descent. As we neared the foot of the mountain we were gladdened by the appearance of a country entirely different from the dark plateau we had crossed. We were surrounded by rolling prairies which were intersected by crystal rivulets; the temperature grew exceedingly mild; here we made a halt to take our meal, and after an hour's repose we were again on our way to Thingvalla.

The lake of Thingvalla is one of the largest of Iceland. Its circumference measures about forty miles. On its borders rise the high and majestic walls of Althing, a spot erected by nature almost into a fortress, where formerly the people held the meetings of their "Thing" or Parliament. In its immediate neighborhood is situated the farmhouse "Thingvalla," where we expected to find a shelter for the night. We had reached the famous "Almannagja," of which Lord Dufferin says that it is worth visiting Iceland were it only to have a sight of this superb scene. In truth, this great rent in the rocks presents one of the wildest and most fantastic aspects. At the entrance we alighted and led our horses by the bridle; for to penetrate into this marvelous chasm we have to descend by a staircase of basalt, hewn by nature itself. Arrived at the bottom, we mount again, to cross this strange passage whose rocky walls rise perpendicular to a giddy height, and are crowned by most extravagant forms in the shape of towers, bastions, minarets, spires, grinning- monsters, hideous spectres, and weird figures. One would indeed fancy that in the dark past some Titans amused themselves here; sculpturing in these rocks this entire freakish design.

Besides its most novel appearance, this spot is of historical interest. Here, according to time-honored traditions, many a bloody battle was fought, the most important of which was the one engaged in between the sons of Njaels, and the mighty Flosi. Snori posted himself with his men at the entrance of the defile, to favor the flight of the sons of Njaels, in case of defeat, or to cut off the retreat of the enemy, should victory smile on them. The "Sagas" relate that, on this memorable occasion, the battle fought between these walls of lava was one of the fiercest.

We soon gained the other end of the chasm. The grandeur of the scene that struck our eyes beggars description. Straight ahead of us stretched the verdant plain of Thingvalla, eight miles broad, and the beautiful lake of the same name. On the left, the waters of the Oxeraa fall, leaping from rock to rock, thus forming a succession of cascades. We advanced to the bank of the river; the ponies plunged into it without the least fear, and waded through the waters up to the shoulders. In the middle of the river we alighted on a small green isle of great historical interest. On this isle, in ancient times, the warlike members of the Althing usually settled their quarrels. Here took place the celebrated duel between "Gumlange Ormsttinga'" and "Ravu'" in the presence of the whole body of the Althing. The victory was adjudged to neither combatant; it was the last combat of the kind, for on the following day, the assembly of the Althing unanimously voted a law prohibiting forever dueling in Iceland.

We delayed but a few moments on this bloodstained islet, so rich in sad memories, and soon gained the opposite bank of the river. Before us rose the "Logberg." From its top all the decisions of tribunals used to be proclaimed and the new laws promulgated, and it was from this spot that, in the year 1000 A.D., the Catholic religion was declared the religion of the state; all the pagans thus had to submit and receive baptism in the waters of the Oxeraa.

As it was already nine o'clock in the evening, and ourselves and the horses were exhausted, we directed our steps straight to the farmhouse of Thingvalla, where we hoped to spend the night; but our hope was to prove unfounded. On the lawn, in front of the house, we perceived a large white tent, and a number of horses grazing. The owner of the property is a Protestant minister; he came to meet us. I asked him whether he could give us hospitality for the night. "I am sorry to say," he answered, "that it is impossible, the house is already crowded with strangers, all the beds are occupied, the men of the farm are obliged to sleep under this tent."

I judged it useless to insist and decided to go on and find a place of rest somewhere else. Just as we were about to depart we noticed a man on horseback who seemed to be in the same plight as ourselves. On Approaching, he saluted us in a friendly manner, and inquired where we were bound. "To the north," I answered. "In this case," said he, "you have to pass near my farm; should you wish we will travel together. If the stranger's room is unoccupied, I shall be happy to offer you hospitality for the night.

We accepted the generous invitation the more readily as we would otherwise have to ride for many an hour before we could enjoy a much needed rest. One thing only made me uneasy; namely, that we had heard nothing of this house; it was not on our list of farms that had been recommended to us, and I did not like to go to a place that was altogether unknown to me. We passed again before the Logberg and the cascade, crossing the Oxeraa River, and skirting the bloody isle. We then turned to the right and ascended a path among rocks. As we proceeded our guide informed us that his farmhouse was called "Skoarket," which means cottage of the woods, and that it was situated on the summit of a mountain about two miles from Thingvalla. "It is," he said, "A humble little dwelling, but we will do our best to make everything as comfortable as possible."

Arriving at the top of the hill we could see the little cottage before us. The kind farmer bid us good bye and galloped ahead to inform his family of our arrival. All the inhabitants of the farm came to meet us, and gave us a most courteous reception. They hastened to take care of our horses and led us into an adjoining building where the guest room was. We admired the holiday garments of the whole family, hanging on the walls. They were red, blue, green, yellow, in fine, all the colors of the rainbow. We asked for some hot water to make a broth with our extract of meat, and we heated a box of canned meat. Our supper was readily prepared; and our host furnished us, according to custom, with fresh milk. The good landlady, a very sprightly little woman, was every now and then at our heels to see whether anything was wanting. How full these people are with kindness and politeness, without ever dreaming of the least remuneration.

After supper we went to see our faithful little horses. We were so far from Reykjavik that I begged our host not to tie their feet; and they did not abuse my confidence. Henceforth, I always let them graze at full liberty. While we were out our beds were prepared. The bedsteads were relics of remotest antiquity. The four heavy columns were coarsely sculptured: the wood had never been painted, but from continual rubbing it shown like a mirror.

The following morning, as soon as we were up we were served, according to custom, with hot coffee and crackers. Our host then invited us to visit his farm of which he seemed very proud. He had introduced many changes and made many improvements, and everything was in exquisite order. The views from the farm were splendid. On one side majestic mountains, on the other Thingvalla and all its marvels—its immense plain, the lake, the Oxeraa River, the celebrated chasm of Almannagja and the roaring cascade. We must confess that the ancient Icelanders chose a superb spot for their assemblies.

Lake Thingvalla, like all the lakes of Iceland, abounds in trout, and this delicate fish is seldom wanting at table. At the farm of " Grunsthinga" the landlady assured us that on the eve of our arrival, the men had caught more than 800 trout in their net, and this in a small lake on the top of the mountain. Two hours later, when they were ready to load their horses with their great catch, they drew the nets again and took at one haul ninety fish.

MT. HEKLA

CHAPTER SEVEN

A TREK TO GEYSER

We were very anxious to reach the Great Geyser, and everything seemed to be in our favor—the weather was superb, there was no wind, and not a cloud visible. We now entered a very fertile country abounding in rich pastures, and flocks of sheep could be seen browsing on the hills and plains. Thus they live during the whole summer in the open air, without any shepherd to guard them, they are only looked after when they approach too near the farms, and then they are driven again to the mountains. Sheep raising is one of the principal industries of Iceland. More than half a million of these animals feed in the inhabited parts of the country. We meet them everywhere—in the valleys, among the rocks, in the plains, on the highest mountains, as far as the eye can reach, even to the edge of the eternal snows. They are all very fat, which proves that the pastures are very rich, and are all horned—a characteristic feature of Icelandic sheep.

After midday, the heat became almost unbearable, both for us and our horses. We found it necessary, successively to lay aside our cloaks, coats, vests, jackets, and thus add a fresh burden to our pack horses, which were already very tired. The thermometer must have been as high as 86° Fahrenheit; but the heat was not the only vexation; for the lake of Thingvalla does not abound in trout exclusively. Myriads of mosquitoes are hatched on its borders, which fill a great space of the neighborhood with their uncalled for music. We were obliged to muffle head and face with handkerchiefs, leaving only the eyes and nose uncovered. We met a caravan; everyone was as lightly dressed like ourselves. They too had to protect themselves against the bloodthirsty mosquitoes, so that we found out that we were not the inventors of the scheme. These troublesome insects prevented us from entering into conversation with the men, according to custom. We simply exchanged a "Saelir verid per!'" and continued our journey in haste.

Here and there the surroundings were charming, and we could not tire contemplating scenes so varied and at times so fairy like. I think one could travel for entire months in this country and ever admire with new delight the magnificent and unparalleled landscapes. Those who have penetrated only a short distance into the interior of the island fancy that there is no variety: but this is decidedly false. The farther you proceed the more you are disabused of this. Every new scene surpasses the preceding and the interest of the tourist is continually kept alive. Of course, this holds true only in the summer months. One of our travelling companions who had crossed Switzerland, Scotland, and Norway, assured us that nothing in these countries can be compared to the natural beauties of Iceland. We met many Englishmen who had visited the island for the third or fourth time, and they told us that they expected to return again.

We continue to ride under this tropical sun. Many a time we had to halt to cool off at some brook before crossing. Finally, after six long hours of riding, we came to a spot which invited us to rest and there we lunched. Unbridling and unsaddling our ponies, we turned them loose upon the pasture, and then sat down in the shade of a gigantic tower of lava. Here we took our meal with great appetite. An hour later we pursued our journey. We were then scarcely half way to our next station. The aspect of the country changed again. We traversed vast plains which stretched out far and wide. At a distance we sighted lake "Langarvatu," which means "lake of boiling springs," It is neither as large nor as beautiful as Lake Thingvalla, but it presents a novel feature. Clusters of vapor columns are continually ascending from it into the sky; the Great Geyser cannot be far.

We hurried past this region of vapor which betrays no little mixture of sulfur. The overwhelming heat is succeeded by an unwholesome freshness. We hasten to put on again the articles of clothing which we had put off some hours before. The mosquitoes had entirely disappeared. We proceed at full speed. Farms appear in every direction; mowers are busy in the meadows. At every path leading to a house, our horses are inclined to turn, but we cannot possibly stop along the road. We strike another river which we must cross. Numberless wild duck are seen everywhere, and flocks of ducklings following their mothers; it was a charming sight.

The sun disappeared behind the glittering glaciers; the fog throws a dark mantle over the surroundings. Our road lies across a kind of pathless desert. Suddenly our horses stopped, seem to deliberate, and refused to proceed. What was the matter? We could see no obstacle. We used the whip freely, but they do not stir; they are trembling all over. We concluded that we were on a dangerous track, doubtless some quagmire, where we might have perished and from which we were only saved by the wonderful instinct of our ponies. We retraced our steps and once on the right path we galloped at full speed, to make up for lost time. Thanks to our faithful steeds, we were all saved, if not from a certain danger, at least from a great discomfort.

It was 8 O'clock in the evening, when we reached the foot of a mountain clad in brushwood; the ascent proved to be very tiresome owing to its steepness. The fog grew thicker as we advanced. Before starting our upward march, I hastened to a farm to inquire about the road. "You cannot reach the Geyser tonight," said they, "but you may follow the mountain road, which is good and even. In four hours you will arrive at Brüarã, and after having crossed a torrent you will come to a farm where you may rest."

I thanked the farmer for the information and wished to leave immediately, but he started, in his turn, to put questions, which I was bound to answer. I then rejoined my companion and we began to climb the mountain. Emerging upon the summit, our horses quickened their pace, and the darker it grew the quicker they ran. At last the darkness became so pronounced that we could not distinguish anything ten or fifteen feet ahead of us. We had to put on our oil-silk suits, for the atmosphere was damp and cold. At the end of a four hours' ride we heard the dull roaring of a torrent; it was the fall of the "Bruara." We spurred on our ponies and soon arrived at its banks. The river is eighty feet broad. Half way across, it is perfectly fordable, but exactly in the middle is a deep cleft, into which the waters from either side fall, and then in a collected volume roar over a precipice a little lower down. Across this cleft some wooden planks have been thrown—the only bridge m Iceland—over which stamping of we were to gain the opposite bank. Our horses hesitate; never had they attempted such a feat. We had much trouble to urge them on. The bridge, especially, which itself was under water, caused them to fear. However, as they seemed to realize there was no other way, they crossed the cascade. We were stunned by the noise of the roaring water.

It is midnight; how we long to meet a dwelling! Every now and then we were deceived by enormous blocks of lava, which, at a distance, appear to be houses. After a good half-hour we see a horse, an infallible sign of the neighborhood of a farm. In fact, five minutes later we perceived a house and hurried to ask hospitality for the night. Unfortunately it contained no guest's room, nothing but what is called an Etuve, and we could not think of sleeping in it.

In Iceland an Etuve is a spacious hall, furnished as in the time of "Harold Haarfager," with big and heavy wooden bedsteads along the walls; the men sleep on one side, and the women on the other.

Sometimes a kind of patrician separates them, but this seldom occurs. The beds accommodate two or more persons; and no one may occupy a bed exclusively for himself; if more strangers wish to lodge at the farm. As long as there is a place left, visitor are welcome to it. This strange custom dates from the Middle Ages, and was common in most of the countries of northern Europe. The insufficiency of ventilation in these dormitories aids much in their discomfort.

"How far is it to the nearest farm?" I inquired. "A Half hour's ride," they answered. As we could not spend the night in the "Etuve" we continued on our way. It took us an hour and a half to find the farm of "Vesturhild," a path across the meadows leading us to it. We arrived at last before the house; everybody was asleep. However, they had heard the stamping of our horses and someone came to the window to see what was the matter. Curiosity soon attracted many more. I saluted them

saying—"Heir de God!" "God be with
you!" They all answered, "God bless you!"
I then asked: "Can you accommodate two
travelers for the night?" They stared at one
another, deliberated among themselves;
finally one of them cried out—"Do you hail
from a foreign land?' "Yes, from
Copenhagen." The consultation was
renewed; several new faces appeared at the
window. They looked at us with evident
curiosity; we must have looked a spectacle to
the angels and to men. Poor little Frederick
was exhausted with fatigue and longing for
rest. I feared lest he should fall asleep on
the saddle, if we had to go farther, and
endeavored to cheer him up. The door
finally opened, and a man approached us
and said: "We have no guest chamber, but
there is still room in the "Etuve,"if you are
pleased with it, you are welcome." "Is it far
from here to the next farm?" I answered.
"Austerhild is at an hour's distance," he
replied, "There you will find a luxurious
room." I made up my mind at once that we
had to at once push on our way.

"Wait a minute," said the farmer. He then rushed to the opposite side of the house and soon reappeared on horseback. Give me the bridle of your pack horse, I will accompany you; it is so dark and you do not know the road." I thanked him heartily and having saluted the crowd at the window we set out in haste. In less than an hour, we arrived at a large and beautiful farm; are guide alighted, climbed the roof and leaned over a small window, he cried out with all his might—"God be with you!" From the interior of the house came the answer— "God bless you!" He leaped from the roof, mounted his horse and bade us goodbye. I experienced some difficulty in making him accept a few coins for the invaluable service he had rendered us. "We are accustomed to help strangers without payment, " said he.

Scarcely had he departed, when a young damsel issued from the house followed by her brother; they approached us, and after the usual salutations, I excused myself for disturbing them in the dead of night.

"Never mind," said she, "this is no inconvenience; our parents will be too happy to extend you hospitality, please wait a moment, I will light a lamp." Her brother took charge of the ponies and soon introduced us into the house. We traversed a spacious vestibule and then entered an elegant little parlor, which we left immediately to put aside our cloaks, all saturated by the heavy fog. On returning we were not a little surprised to find the apartment furnished like the parlors of Copenhagen. A fine carpet covered the floor, in the centre a little round table and a sofa, along the walls a library and several pieces of mahogany furniture; everything was scrupulously neat and orderly. It was far past midnight, and as we had tasted nothing since midday, our hostess prepared supper for us to which our hunger gave the relish of a royal banquet. Our beds were gotten ready in two separate rooms. They asked us to choose between down coverlets and woolen blankets; we preferred the latter, for the weather was very mild.

We enjoyed a refreshing sleep, and awoke very late in the day; the sun darted its warm and brilliant rays into the rooms when we opened our eyes. After coffee we set out to admire the beautiful landscape. Before us stretched imposing mountains; beneath, a delightful valley; in the background, glaciers of dazzling whiteness, and in their midst Mt. Hekla crowned with ice and snow. The mountains, glaciers and valleys, had assumed new traits of beauty, owing to the fine weather which followed the fog of yesterday; the air was embalmed with the perfume of wild mountain flowers. On the right we could see Hankadalen and the Great Geyser, smoking and roaring.

GEYSER

CHAPTER EIGHT

THE GREAT GEYSER

We departed from Austerhild in the afternoon, and had been hardly two hours riding when we reached the farm of Lang, situated about 800 feet from the Great Geyser; here dwells Sigurdr of Lang. He is eighty years old, strong and alert for his age. His great kindness to all has become a byword in Iceland. He owns three farms south of the Geyser. Two years ago, to the evident mortification of the Icelanders, he sold the Geyser, which was his property, to an Englishman, for the paltry sum of $15,000. The intention of the purchaser is to surround it with a high wall in order to tax every pilgrim who wishes to get a look at it. Really the Englishmen are shrewd merchants! This explains a rumor we heard at Reykjavik. An agent of an English firm had landed there to make arrangements with the local authorities about building a railway from the capital to the Geyser. A line of steamers would ply conjointly between Liverpool and Iceland. They agreed to pay $20,000 a year for the land, for the space of thirty years, after which the railway would be their property. The work was to be begun in 1895.

As nobody appeared around the house, I dismounted and with a stick struck the wall near the entrance three times. This is, during the day, the conventional announcement of the arrival of strangers; at night, one must climb the roof and shout at the window, "God be with you!" to which comes invariably the answer, "God bless you!" Scarcely had I complied with this usage, when a woman opened the door and saluted us. I asked her whether I could speak to the master of the house; she disappeared at once to call him. I wished to beg Sigurdr to kindly guide us to "Kallmanstunga" a farm situated in the midst of a desert on the opposite side of the mountain before us. It required an eight hours' ride over a great stony sea of lava, during which time not a house nor a blade of grass was to be found. Our greatest danger, however, lay in the crossing of the thirteen branches of the rapid river Hvita. No one dares engage in this undertaking without a sure and experienced guide. But three men can boast of guiding you safely through this dangerous part of the country; namely, Sigurdr of Lang, his son Greipr of Hankadalr, and Gudjön, a farmer of the neighborhood. In spite of his advanced age, Sigurdr is the best of the trio. The gentleman accosted us in a friendly manner. He is a man of a noble and imposing manner, with a snow-white beard. I saluted him; he stared at me without answering, then he bent over a little boy who accompanied him; the child shouted into his ear: "The gentleman salutes you— Saelir verid per!"

Sigurdr then said, "Welcome, my friends!" "I come to beg you, " I cried with all my might," to accompany us to Kallmanstunga!" I had not spoken loud enough, so the child repeated my words. The old man thought a moment and answered: "I fear I am not able to render you this service, but my son Greipr will most readily accompany you; and if he cannot, I will go with you." He then took me by the arm and asked a thousand questions, to answer which I yelled myself hoarse. When this lung and throat exercise was over, he told the boy to lead us to the Geyser to show us the environs, and then to guide us to Hankadalr where his son Greipr lives.

We were, therefore, to contemplate, for the first time, the Great Geyser. We soon reached the foot of a round rocky hill; from its summit arose thick columns of vapor presenting the appearance of a dozen factory chimneys; the air was impregnated with a nauseous odor resembling sulphurated hydrogen, a great subterraneous noise was heard, like that of boiling water; for the water is always boiling in these immense stone vessels. The boy walked before us showing the way as we ascended to the basin of the Geyser. Our horses began to show signs of fear; they scented the rocks on which they stepped and finally refused to advance. Pricking up their ears, they looked about in great anxiety. We were forced to use the whip to urge them forward, but they only dragged on with great precaution and appeared thoroughly frightened. Having reached a certain height we saw before us a round opening about the size of our Amagatoro at Copenhagen, whence escaped a dense vapor which rose to a great height. Our ponies stared at this strange spectacle for a few seconds, when, overcome by fear, they deliberately wheeled around. We could not keep them quiet, so we were forced to dismount and lead them by the bridle. Passing several of these steaming orifices we pushed on till we reached the Great Geyser. The rocks about these geysers are burning hot, while the ground around is of the ordinary temperature. These seething rocks produce a hissing sound like steam escaping from an engine. Our horses became more and more terrified and walked as if they were treading on burning coals. Finally, we reach the Great Geyser. A smooth stone basin, seventy-two feet in diameter, and four feet deep, stood before us, brimful of boiling clear water, which bubbled up more violently in the centre than at the edges. I dipped my finger lightly into it; but even this slight contact left a burning mark. Several scientists have taken the temperature of this water. On the surface it indicates 185° Fahrenheit while at a depth of sixty feet it rises to 250°. We longed to see an eruption of the Great Geyser, but we were sadly disappointed. Our guide wondered at the interest we took in this unparalleled phenomenon of nature. He was born in its neighborhood, saw it daily and had witnessed many a violent manifestation of wrath of this monster. I asked whether it was safe to stay so near the basin, as, in case of an eruption we would have a rather disagreeable showering bath of boiling water. "Oh," he answered, "it does not occur without a warning. Before the water bursts into the air, subterraneous thunders accompanied by earthquakes, admonish you to look for a safe spot which you find in going against the wind." I further inquired how the eruption takes place. He replied: "The whole mass of water lifts itself up and rises like a column into the air, sometimes 200 feet. This action is repeated four or five times successively. Most of the water falls back into the basin, except in times of strong wind; the rest turns into vapor and scatters." "When did such an eruption last take place?" I asked. "Last night." He replied. "Does it happen often?" I continued. "Oh! The fits are very ill regular; sometimes they occur two or three times a day, sometimes once in three weeks; but last spring the eruptions occurred almost every twenty-four hours."

Afterwards, we visited the smaller geysers. The most remarkable of these is the Strokr. Its water boils more violently than that of the Great Geyser; so that its groaning and hissing could be heard at a distance. The orifice of the Strokr measures only six feet in diameter. As it has no basin, we could approach to the very edge of its funnel, which is smoothly hollowed out of a red rock, and look down at the water boiling perpetually at the bottom. We found it impossible to lead our horses to this geyser for the noise and vapor made them shiver.

ICELANDIC FARM LIFE

CHAPTER NINE

HOSPITALITY AT HANKADALR

After having satisfied our curiosity we directed our steps to Hankadalr where we wished to spend the night. We forded a river in which our horses got a cold bath, for the water reached to their shoulders. At Hankadalr we gave the conventional sign of three strokes against the wall, which instantly brought out farmer Greipr. He is a tall, strong young man. He received us with the utmost politeness, especially when he learned that we came from his father's house. We were conducted into the guest's room, which was simply furnished and exquisitely neat. Our bedsteads consisted of trunks placed side by side, the sheets and coverlets were rather rough. Our host served us the best he had.

In the evening as we were sitting on the lawn in front of the house, chatting and enjoying the fine scenery, suddenly we saw a

man on horseback galloping towards us. It
was not long before recognizing old Sigurdr
himself, and we rose to meet him. Having
alighted, the old man affectionately
embraced his son. He had come to ascertain
whether his son would be able to
accompany us the next day to
Kallmanstunga. They held a protracted
consultation together. It seems that Greipr
had never travelled over more than half the
road, and we needed a guide who was
perfectly acquainted with the whole; for
should a fog overtake tis on the mountains,
we might easily stray from our path and thus
be exposed to spend one or two nights
without a shelter. It was, therefore, decided
that Greipr should ask Gudjön to
accompany us, and if he could not do so,
Sigurdr himself would be our guide. After
this, he bid us good night and returned
home.

A message was accordingly sent to
Gudjön, but he was absent; thus we were
forced to stay at Hankadalr the whole of the

following day. We profited by this delay to visit the environs and to make a collection of minerals for our museum of Ordrupshoj. This part of Iceland abounds in hot springs, many of which still bear their Old Catholic names. Near the farm is St. Martin's spring; the landlady uses its clear and healthy water for kitchen purposes, and she keeps there her kettles and some pans. The good people of the village also come to this spring to prepare their meals, and thus spare wood and coal, the subterraneous fire renders them service gratis; winter and summer. I put a box of canned meat into this water and after a quarter of an hour we enjoyed a good repast. Near this crater, a basin has been dug into which the boiling water flows. Here is soon cools down, and in winter the water is frozen everywhere else, the cattle come to drink it.

While here we had an opportunity to observe the love the Icelanders have for their horses. At midday the oldest boy went to drive in a dozen ponies in order to feed them on hay. We all left the house with the children. Scarcely were the ponies in sight when they ran to meet them crying out; "Oh, the dear little creatures!" The ponies stepped forward with the greatest care for fear of treading on the children, who hung about them caressing them and calling each one by his name. After the meal, they leaped on the horses and galloped off. One pony did not follow the crowd but ran to the entrance of the house, stuck his head inside and began to stamp. "He wants his milk," said one of the children that stood near him. The landlady soon appeared with a small pail of sheep milk and gave it to the pony. She told me that she bought the animal when a foal and raised it on sheep milk, to which he became so accustomed that every day, at this hour, he came to the house for it.

In the afternoon we visited the greatest waterfall of Iceland, named "Kellegulfoss." Here the river Hvita tumbles its mass of water down a lofty precipice. The roaring of the torrent can be heard from afar, and at several miles distant a column of spray can be seen curling about the fall.

When we returned to the house, Frederick played hide-and-seek with the children; I was readily struck by the ease with which children make friends; later on Frederick organized games of hide-and-seek at every farm we stopped at, to the great joy of the parents and amusement of the children. Nowhere was he in want of companions, for Iceland swarms with children in this part. Meanwhile old Sigurdr and his son succeeded in finding our guide; he asked five dollars for his service, the usual fee, for he was to lose two days and he had to use two horses on account of the difficulties and fatigues of the journey. It was decided that we should leave at 6 O'clock in the morning.

The next day, before leaving, I wished to settle accounts with our host, but he refused all payment, although we had spent two days and two nights at his house. After much entreaty I succeeded in making him accept a small sum for which he and his wife thanked me with many expressions of gratitude. Everywhere in Iceland the good people of the country look upon hospitality as a sacred duty, and treat as best they can all those the Lord sends them. I was grieved to hear that sometimes travelers behave rudely towards their charitable hosts. A landlady said to me: "Oh, the strangers are never satisfied with our services. They complain of not being better treated, and of getting bad food; they accuse us of uncleanliness and of charging too much for their board. Once we asked fifty cents a head; they found the price exorbitant, and yet we lost a day's work and gave them the best we possessed." These exacting tourists do not reflect on what the least article costs these poor people. Coffee, sugar, flour, oil, in a word, everything, has to be brought from a great distance on the backs of horses.

Between 6 and 7 O'clock we left Hankadalr with five horses. As we ascended the nearest mountain, we saw the Great Geyser in eruption. What a mortification not to be nearer! Our road was now the worst imaginable; sometimes we faced a steep ascent up a high mountain; then a rugged descent into a deep valley; again we cut across a bleak desert strewn with big stones, afterward we climbed another mountain. Thus we trudged along the whole day. We traversed the valley Kaldadal, locked up between two imposing glaciers which skirt the path, so that we rode in the snow. The weather, however, was superb. This slow and laborious locomotion had lasted about fourteen hours when at 9 O'clock in the evening we struck an even path on which we could ride at a fair rate. Again we had to slacken our speed to descend into a broad valley. We reached the ford of the river Hvita between 1 and 2 O'clock A. M.

Our readers will remember that at this season there is no night in this northern region, the sun scarcely goes below the horizon. We gazed in astonishment upon this torrent which hurled its foamy waters over numberless rocks. Our guide stopped, examined the river and said—"It is impossible to cross at this spot; it is too dangerous." We then skirted the river for a while and made another halt. Our guide tried first to cross the torrent alone with his best pony. In spite of the repeated application of the whip, the poor animal refused to plunge into this icy water; but he finally yielded and walked into the river till the water reached his shoulders. The current dragged him along; suddenly he sank into a hole and his head alone appeared above the surface; he was wet to the belt. Happily the pony succeeded in gaining a footing, but only to retrace his steps. Gudjön betrayed some embarrassment, and proposed to continue along the river until we found a more favorable ford. After a short time we made another trial, but without success. The horse could not withstand the current; the ford was too uneven. With much effort and with great difficulty did he succeed in returning.

We then went further up the river in search of a more fordable place. Our brave guide, fatigued and soaked as he was, did not lose heart. He tried a third time, and was lucky enough to reach the opposite bank. He returned immediately and took Frederick on his own horse; the poor beast had again to fight against the violent current. In the middle of the river he sank into a hole, but happily extricated himself in a moment. Frederick alighted and Gudjön returned to take me across. He made me mount his horse and he leaped upon mine. We tied the others together by the bridle and he took the lead while I closed up the file. For a while we were carried along by the current, but arriving in the middle of the river we were better able to resist its violence and we touched the bank without any other accident.

More than ever we experienced the strength and safety of our dear little Icelandic horses. We were told that these ponies are never drowned, and if the riders know how to cling to them, they need have no fear in crossing rivers; the danger is less than it appears. Those who meet with serious accidents are either under the influence of liquor or rashly hazarding a crossing at a place where the torrent is too deep, and where the horses are obliged to swim with the riders on their backs. We traversed the twelve other branches of the river without further incident.

After this we journeyed through a barren pathless desert. Our guide did not know the exact situation of the farm of Kallmanstunga, so we were forced to search for it. To our great joy at 3 O'clock. A. M., we suddenly found ourselves on a fine lawn; we were at Kallmanstunga. We alighted. Our guide climbed the roof of the house and cried: "Her voere Gud!" And the answer came—"God bless you!" Without delay the door was opened and a cordial reception awaited us. Throughout the rest of our journey we experienced the same cordiality and courtesy wherever we stopped.

We stayed a whole day at Kallmanstunga to rest ourselves and our ponies, as we had a hard and fatiguing journey before us. It is useless to describe our sojourn at Kallmanstunga, as it varies little from the one at Hankadalr.

Our next station was Grimstunga. To reach it we had to traverse the Arnarvatusheide, a magnificent tract of land with great natural beauty, but entirely uninhabited. We were lucky enough to meet two travelers who were going in the same direction—a student of Reykjavik, and an elderly lady. The young man had made this trip several times and he assured us that he knew the road perfectly.

We rose at 3 O'clock A.M. Before leaving we asked our host how much we owed him; he answered, "$3 75." This was the only place where the price was mentioned. We set out, hoping to arrive at Grimstunga about 1 O'clock P. M., should there happen no accident. Our host accompanied us for three hours, to direct us to the best ford of the river Nordlunga. Sometimes we beheld immense rocks rising vertically to a height of more than 5000 feet, whose ice crowned summits sparkled with a thousand fires beneath the rays of the setting sun; then we descried lofty blue mountains, studded with crystal lakes, on which flocks of snow-white swan were sporting. At midday we took an hour's rest on the shore of one of these lakes, into which leaped a magnificent cascade. On resuming our journey our guide, mistaking the path, led us by a circuitous road through a wild desert, so that instead of arriving at Grimstunga at 1 P. M. we arrived at 5 A. M. the following day. The people had already risen when we neared the farm.

CHAPTER TEN

THE ONLY

CATHOLICS IN ICELAND

The reception tendered us at Grimstunga was most cordial! Our host helped us to take off our overcoats and our dirty boots, and then offered us a drink of warm milk. Shortly after an excellent breakfast was served, consisting of trout, meat, vegetables, delicious bread and fresh butter, and rhubarb preserves, seasoned with sweet cream. The owner of Grimstunga is a wealthy gentleman and a representative of this part of the island in Congress. Soon after we retired to bed for a well-deserved rest. We rose late in the afternoon and felt entirely refreshed. We spent the night at Grimstunga to give more time to our horses to recuperate, because their backs were sore and raw. No guide was henceforth needed as our road ran through the luxuriant plains of fertile valleys dotted with cozy farm houses. I will be brief on this part of my trip lest I prolong too much an already lengthy narrative. The farmers of the North in general enjoy comfort and wealth and can easily afford being generous to strangers. We are glad to say that a large share of that generosity was lavished upon us.

The following day we bade farewell to our kind hosts and entered the picturesque Vastursdal. This valley lies between two chains of mountains; through the centre flows a large river, with numerous houses on its banks. Wherever we turn we can see the mowers cutting the grass on the meadows. We stopped over night at a farm named Karusa. We were cordially welcomed by the owner of the place, a young theological student of the college of Reykjavik, who lives in a fine two-story building. He put a suite of four apartments at our disposal—a parlor, dining- room, and two sleeping rooms, each furnished with a large English bed. This young gentleman and his sister, who keeps house for him, spared no pains to make us feel at home. I intimated that our saddles needed repairs; immediately a saddler was called who did the job very neatly. Before leaving, the hostess gave Frederick a box of candy. Such a gift can only be appreciated when one remembers with what difficulties these articles are procured. No entreaties could make them accept the least remuneration. "Our mother strictly forbade us," said the gentleman, "to receive any payment from those who ask for hospitality." We were not even allowed to pay for the repairs of our saddles. Later on I learned that this family was in rather moderate circumstances.

After heartily thanking our hosts for their extreme kindness, we set out in company with the young student who wished to guide us to the farm "Huansum" where we intended to pass the night. On reaching Huansum our worthy companion introduced us to the owner of the place who welcomed us most politely. He was a well-educated gentleman who had travelled a great deal and was an entertaining conversationalist. Here I slept the first time in what they called a "closed bed." A similar article can be seen in the Museum of Northern Antiquities, at Copenhagen.

Our host's son escorted us a great distance, for we had to cross a chain of mountains. The boy bid us farewell when we could see the farm "Solheimar," our next station. We rode by the side of a charming lake several miles long but very narrow. It reminded us of Loch Lomond, in the mountains of Scotland, with this difference, that the latter is surrounded by beautiful woods, while around the former there is no sign of a tree. At Solheimar we were sumptuously entertained.

Today we were to tread the valley for the last time, first crossing the torrent Blanda, which is much deeper than the Hvita, where we had to undergo so great fatigues, and then riding over a chain of mountains. This stretch would bring us to the farm "Vidimyri," by sunset. The farmer of Solheimar ordered a boy to help us to cross the Blanda. On nearing the bank of the river the boy ascended a knoll and cried with all his might, "ferja!" "Ferry-boat!" Our guide had to yell again and again before he could be heard. The echo of the mountains repeated without end, "ferja!" Finally we noticed an old man coming down a neighboring hill and advancing slowly in our direction; he was the ferryman. His voice was very harsh, and his strength seemed prodigious. He placed our saddles and boxes in the boat and then drove the ponies into the river, where they were obliged to swim. Shortly before reaching Vidimyri we found ourselves on the coast facing the isle of Drasig, so renowned for the exploits of Gretta. It is an enormous rock rising perpendicularly above the wave at a short distance from the shore. There lived for twenty years the outlaw Gretta, and there he was surprised by his enemies and assassinated after a bold resistance. We were treading upon the spot where his head was buried by the murderers.

From Vidimyri we went to Silfrastathir. Between these two farms lies a very deep river having several branches. One of these, called "Heradsvotnin," the horses swam, and we crossed it on a boat, the others, we forded. Once we found it difficult to discover the ford. We saw a little girl on the opposite bank. We called her and inquired where we could cross. She directed her pony to where we stood and told us to follow her. We did so without hesitation, and gained the opposite bank without difficulty. On such occasions the usual word exchanged is "Happy journey!" but in these parts of Iceland, intersected by torrents and rivers, they say: "Good River!" With this wish the girl galloped off. We arrived safely at Silfrastathir and stayed the night.

Around Silfrastathir the scenery was beautiful, our path leading us through the picturesque defiles of the Oscnadal. In the afternoon we were rowed over the deep river Horgara which waters the fertile Horgarasdal valley, and came to the farm of Modruvollum, which is well known throughout the country. Madame Stephensen, the lady of the house, gave us a cordial reception. Modruvollum is the most important farm we met on our trip and there is an excellent school attached to it. The children were then on vacation.

Madame Stephensen ordered a servant to guide us to Hjalteyei, our last station. It is a little merchant town situated at the extreme end of the beautiful bay of Ofjord. Here lives Gunnar Einarsson, with his family, the only Catholics of Iceland. If one remembers that they have the consolations of our holy religion but every other year, he will easily conceive the great joy this faithful little flock experiences on the arrival of a priest in their midst. We had eight days to stay with them;

a time of grace for these dear brothers in the faith, so abandoned in this forlorn place. The best apartment of the house was immediately turned into a chapel. Each day I said Mass, and preached on the principal truths of our holy religion, and each member of the family approached the sacraments several times with touching fervor.

Never shall I forget the kindness and reverence with which I was treated by this excellent family. I have described the generous hospitality we enjoyed from those who were not of our faith; it would be impossible to give an adequate idea of the affectionate welcome we experienced from our Catholic brethren. It was therefore with reluctance that we tore ourselves away from them on August 23, to hasten to Akureyri, whence the steamer "Thyra" was to take us back to Copenhagen. At Akureyri we disposed of our ponies, which had rendered us such good services. Thanks to our host Gunnar, who accompanied us, we sold them very advantageously. The "Thyra" was late. Gunnar however did not leave us until he had seen us safe on board the steamer.

AKUREYRI

CHAPTER ELEVEN

DEPARTURE AT AKUREYRI

On the Thyra we met several of our former traveling companions, all of whom were much pleased with their stay in Iceland, and a great number of them desired to return again. We related our numerous adventures, and listened with attention to theirs. Our seventeen days' trip on horseback had seemed an extraordinary feat, but we stopped boasting when we learned that some of our friends had been three, and even five consecutive weeks scouring the country on little ponies. All looked healthy and were delighted with the benefits they reaped during their short stay in this happy clime. I was very glad to meet an English Catholic priest on board—the professor of canon law and moral theology at Oscott College. Before his trip he suffered so much from insomnia that he was rendered unfit for work. His physician advised him to make an excursion to Iceland, and this completely restored him to health. All the tourists said that there was no place like Iceland to regain health and strength of body, especially if the summer is always as beautiful as it is this year. I am afraid, however, that this is not the case.

Travelling in Iceland has a charm of its own, unknown elsewhere. The daily riding, the varied scenes, the objects of interest—all break the monotony and routine experienced in a trip by rail. Even Scotland, with its mountains, lakes and forests, has lost by the introduction of modern comforts, and by the profuse description of every nook and corner. Here you travel always in the open air, behold remarkable scenery, and are continually led from surprise to surprise. Frederick and I could judge of the difference between these two countries, having extensively travelled together over Scotland, the preceding year. There we travelled in comfortable cars, steamboats carried us across the lakes, tramways took us up the mountains and everywhere sumptuous hotels with all their luxuries were opened to us. In Iceland there are no hotels, no railways, no steamers, no noise nor smoke, except the low grumbling of the geysers and the vapor of the hot springs.

You breathe the purest and most invigorating air and enjoy the greatest liberty. You start and stop where you please, you rest as long as you please; there is no ticket to be bought, no time-table to be followed, no darkness to be dreaded, for the sun does not set in summer. As for food, you get your provisions beforehand, moreover, you are always warmly welcomed by the good people of the country and invited to share their frugal repast. Sometimes you may lunch sitting on a green knoll, and for drink you have the purest water in the world, for the spring water of Iceland, as a Danish physician affirms, is so remarkable for its purity and health-giving properties that it would pay to bottle it for transportation   In many locations it has a strong taste.

We steamed out of Ofjord Bay August 26th, and coasted for several days stopping at half a dozen harbors and fiords to receive passengers and merchandise. Every night the firmament was illumined by the splendors of the aurora borealis. Among the passengers we counted about a hundred inhabitants of the Faroe Islands, who, after fishing on the coasts of Iceland for two months, were returning home. They were a jolly set, full of good humor, and every evening they sang some of the touching national melodies for which their country is famous.

At the Faroes I again visited the old lady at Hvidernaes, celebrated Mass in her home, and gave her Holy Communion, though the captain allowed me scarcely more time than at our first visit. From the Faroes we sailed to Edinburgh; then to Copenhagen where we landed September 6th, late in the evening; at half-past ten we boarded the train for Klompenborg and at midnight reached home—our college at Ordrupshoj.

ABOUT THE AUTHOR

This thrilling story "A Journey Across Iceland" was written by the famous Icelandic author of children's books and Jesuit Jón Sveinsson* (up to now the only Icelandic Jesuit). He was born on November 16, 1857, at the farmstead Möðruvellir in North Iceland. When he was a boy his nickname was "Nonni" and that is why the 12 books about his adventures and experiences are called the "Nonni books." During the twentieth century readers of all ages throughout the world devoured the stories of his adventures and the Nonni books became bestsellers—published in approximately 40 languages.

Before Jón Sveinsson became a writer he traveled throughout Europe giving many talks about his adventures in his fascinating Icelandic motherland – the country of ice and fire. Children and grown-ups filled large lecture halls and listened breathlessly to the charismatic Icelander. With his white beard and kind blue eyes the tall man himself was an impressive figure who caught everyone's attention. He loved children and they loved him in return. They even sent him letters begging to be taken along on his journeys. His readers could scarcely wait for his next book to appear.

May this book's trip through the United States, Canada, and other English speaking countries be as successful as Nonni's first visit to the "new world" in 1936 when Jón Sveinsson arrived in New York by steamship. This was the first stop of his trip around the world at the age of 80 years instead of taking 80 days as in Jules Verne's famous science fiction story!

On his North American trip he was a guest of Fordham University for three months. He then traveled to Winnipeg where he visited his youngest brother Friðrik and other Icelandic immigrants to

Canada from Akureyri that he knew before he left Iceland as a 12-year-old boy in the autumn of 1870. The last stop in North America was San Francisco where he had been invited to stay at the university. After two months Nonni continued his world trip and traveled across the Pacific Ocean on a Japanese steamship to visit Sophia University in Tokyo for a year. There he was the guest of Fr. Hermann Heuvers S.J., the second president of the university.

In 1938 Nonni returned to Europe via China, the Indian Ocean, the Red Sea, through the Suez Canal on to Gibraltar, and finally back to London. After resting from the long journey Jón Sveinsson started to write two very interesting and fascinating books in German about his trip around the world, namely "Nonni in Amerika," and "Nonni in Japan." He finished writing the first one but unfortunately could only complete 39 chapters of "Nonni in Japan" before his departure on his last trip—to heaven. His lifelong friend Hermann Krose added the chapters 40 – 44 after studying Nonni's detailed diaries and Herder published the books posthumously. Nonni died peacefully on October 16, 1944 at the age of 87 in Cologne, Germany, and was buried there in the Melaten Cemetery.

*The author's Icelandic name is "Jón Sveinsson" but he changed it to "Svensson" once he started writing his books in German. He feared that his German readers might mispronounce his surname. Thus his "nom de plume" has become "Svensson" except in Iceland.

A Pilgrimage to Iceland

by John Vilhelmsson

After the sudden loss of his father a son recalls a trip they had planned to make together. A trip to his father's homeland of Iceland some fifty years after he had left. In his sorrow the son decides to set out upon the journey alone in order to honor his father's memory. To set out upon a pilgrimage to Iceland.

This true story features many photos. A unique combination of personal, philosophical, and spiritual reflections this book's sense of immediacy and wonder seeks to literally bring the reader along on the adventure, while its sense of reverence for the Icelandic culture, land, and people sets it apart from other tales of Iceland. This is Iceland as seen both through the mind and through the heart.

All Chaos To Order Publishing books are in easy to read large print. Please visit us at www.c2op.com

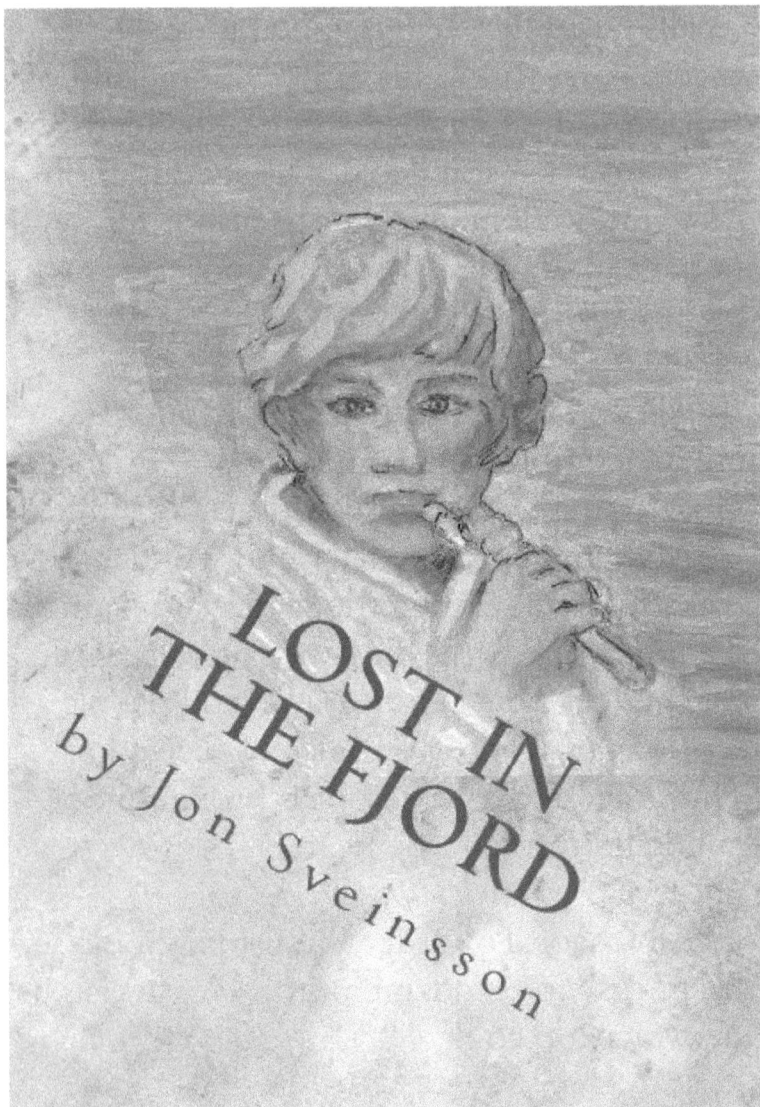

LOST IN
THE FJORD
by Jon Sveinsson

Nonni and his younger brother Manni are Icelandic boys who live in the charming town of Akureyri which sits by the Eyjafjörður Fjord in northern Iceland. Nonni is curious about many things yet forgetful of his parents' warnings, while Manni is quite innocent and pure of heart and loyal toward Nonni. Thinking he can lure the fish out of the sea with his magic flute playing Nonni, with trusting Manni at his side, sets out upon the Eyjafjörður Fjord in a small row boat in order to try. Great adventures follow in this classic and true story of virtue and vocation. Pacific Book Review's "Best Children's Book" of 2014! (Fully illustrated and in large print).